A Pack of Wolves

Written by Vicki

Contents

CELEBRATION PRESS
Pearson Learning Group

The Gray Wolf

Large numbers of gray wolves once lived in North America. For years, humans and wolves shared the land. Early hunters admired the wolf's skill. Then people started to farm, build cities, and raise cattle. They wanted to protect their cattle and pets. They killed about nine out of every ten wolves. That's why today, wolves have disappeared from most states.

Wolves are the largest members of the dog family. There are five types of gray wolves found in North America. They are the eastern timber, Great Plains, Rocky Mountain, Mexican, and Arctic wolves. Adult gray wolves can weigh between 50 and 145 pounds. Males tend to be larger than females. Gray wolves' fur ranges in color from white to gray to black. Their bushy tails are about 2 feet long. In cold climates, a wolf curls its tail around its nose for warmth when it rests.

Wolves have very good senses. With their yellow eyes, they can spot a rabbit trying to hide 400 yards away. Wolves can hear mice under the ground with their large, pointed ears. Their sense of smell is amazing, too. When the wind is just right, a wolf can sniff out its prey about a mile away. ✱

Rocky Mountain wolf

Mexican wolf

Great Plains wolf

Eastern timber wolf

Arctic wolf

Life in a Pack

Gray wolves live in packs of about 6 to 15 wolves. Traveling in packs helps them to hunt larger animals. A moose, for example, can be ten times bigger than a wolf, but a pack of wolves can kill this large beast.

A pack of wolves **roams** over the same area, year after year. Some areas can be more than 500 square miles. Each pack defends its land against other wolf packs. As wolves patrol their land, they mark their borders by spraying their scent on trees, rocks, and bushes. Their howls also warn other packs to "keep out!"

Gray wolves live in packs of 6 to 15 wolves.

While playing, wolves teach each member its rank in the pack.

Wolves are known for their howls. They howl to keep the pack together when on the move. They howl at the start of a chase and just for fun. The sound of howling can carry for miles. When one wolf howls, others in the pack return the cry. Each wolf howls a different note.

A wolf pack has a social order. Pack members play and work together. They also take care of their young. The strongest of the pack is the leader. Other members are the **offspring** of the lead pair and sometimes the leader's brothers and sisters. Every wolf has a **rank** in the pack. Wolves' ranks are often worked out while fighting, playing, or eating.

The lead wolf has many jobs. It leads the hunt, divides the food, and **settles** fights. After a kill, the leader eats first. Then, the other wolves eat in order of their rank in the pack. Wolves are very loyal and caring with each other. They usually obey their leader. When they don't, the lead wolf growls or **nips** their neck.

How Wolves Hunt

Wolves hunt often. They work together to catch large prey, such as deer or **elk**. Wolves are known for their attacks. First, the pack chases its prey. Then it can attack one of the animals. Sometimes one wolf goes for the throat while others grab the rear legs.

Wolves work together to catch large prey.

Hunting is very hard work for wolves. They may travel more than 10 miles to hunt one animal. Often their prey is big, fast, and hard to bring down. Many times the prey escapes. When wolves kill a big animal, they stuff themselves. Each wolf eats up to 20 pounds of meat. After a nap, they may eat again. If there are leftovers, they are often buried for later. In order for the pack to survive, it needs to kill about one large animal per week.

Wolves aren't too picky about food. In the summer or when big game is scarce, they hunt alone to catch mice, beaver, and rabbits. When salmon move upstream, wolves will go fishing. Sometimes they eat dead game and will fight other animals for it.

Parenting: A Group Effort

Gray wolves tend to pick mates for life. In most packs, only the lead pair mates and has pups. Other members may try to mate—only to get punished by the leaders.

Each spring, when the female is pregnant, she looks for a den near fresh water. Sometimes she digs deep tunnels that lead into her den. With the pack outside, the female gives birth to a litter of four to six pups. Wolf pups are born blind and deaf. The mother wolf cleans each 1-pound baby and then puts it to her side to **nurse**. Young pups are dependent on their mothers. After about 3 weeks, the growing pups are able to see, hear, walk, and make noise.

Young pups are dependent on their mother.

Each member of the pack helps to raise the young pups. They take turns watching and playing with the new pups. After a kill, the adult wolves gulp down meat and then return to the den to feed the pups. They spit up chunks of food as the pups lick their mouth. After about 6 months, the pups are strong enough to join the pack for hunting trips.

More than half of the pups die before they're a year old. They die from accidents, diseases, starvation, and attacks from **predators**.

Protecting Wolves

Gray wolves are still considered a **threatened** species.
People who value wolves are working to save them. There
are 13 states actively trying to protect wolves. In 1995, the
U.S. Fish and Wildlife Service set about 30 wolves free in
Yellowstone National Park. At first, **ranchers** and farmers
were upset. They thought the wolves would kill their
livestock and hurt their businesses. To keep peace, the
government pays for livestock killed by wolves.

This gray wolf is being set free in Yellowstone National Park.

It is important to protect wolves and the areas where they live. Without wolves, the number of deer, moose, and elk can become too large. As a great predator, wolves help to keep nature in balance.

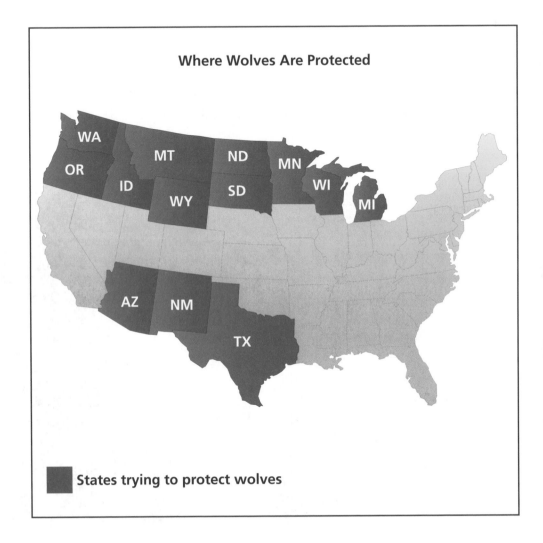

Where Wolves Are Protected

States trying to protect wolves

Glossary

elk   large deer

livestock   the cows and other animals owned by a farmer or rancher

nips   lightly bites

nurse   how female wolves feed their newly born pups

offspring   the wolves born of adult wolves

predators   animals that kill and eat other animals

ranchers   people who raise large numbers of animals, such as cows, horses, and sheep

rank   position; importance

roams   travels about

settles   decides

threatened   in danger of dying out